For Daws to Peck At

Monk Gibbon

FOR DAWS TO PECK AT

" But I will wear my heart upon my sleeve
For daws to peck at "

LONDON
VICTOR GOLLANCZ LIMITED
14 Henrietta Street Covent Garden
1929

TO THAT COURAGEOUS GIRL
MY WIFE

Printed in Great Britain by
The Camelot Press Ltd., London and Southampton

CONTENTS

PR6013
.I 23
F6
1929b

DISPOSSESSED POET

I am from Ireland,
The sad country,
Born, as can be proved,
In her chief city.
When I was a child,
I heard much slander
Touching her, from goose
And hissing gander.
When I was a youth,
A war sent me
Two seas off from her,
In longing twenty.
It was there I found
A taste for roaming,
As in summers hot
Bees do for swarming.
No land sees me now
Five moons or longer,
Even she who reared
Proves little stronger.
I have lost her speech ;
Her men would count me
Stranger if I spoke,
Not of their country.
I have lost her ways,
Her thought, her murmur ;
I have lost all
But my love for her.

THE WISE LOVER

He who loves beauty wisely
Loves her least touch ;
She can scourge him with arrows
Who loves too much ;
Who turns aside, who lingers,
Who leaves the throng,
She can scourge him with scorpions
Who loves too long.

APRIL

Small clouds across the sun,
And a blue sky,
And a strong wind, and then
My love comes by.

And at once I say to her,
" Let's walk again,
Round by the further cliffs,
And risk the rain.

" For clouds blow swift, you know,
A day like this,
And the wind's clean and fresh
Like a child's kiss.

" And the sun's bright and strong,
And very clear—
More clear than when the month
Of June is here."

Does she believe me then ?
Her smile is all
The answer that I get,
And where the wall

Rounds the sea-path we walk,
And I can see
The blue sky of her eyes,
And a grey sea.

And watch her hair blown back
From off her brow,
And talk to her and love
Her silence now.

For she hardly speaks at all,
But lets me see
The sweetness in her face
Quite silently.

And I feel the spray on my own
When I look away,
Fearing to frighten her—
(For eyes can say

More than the heart must tell,
Or words dispatch,
Or ears give credence to,
Or even catch.)

What of it all, you ask,
Who know the way
Round that sea-path we went
Not yesterday.

Did it keep fine for us,
The sun remain ?
The clouds grow still more few,
And cheat the rain ?

Or did the clouds collect,
Before we turned,
And steal five minutes more
Of all I'd earned ?

And rain come down and spoil
My happiness,
And drive us home again,
And spoil her dress ?

I have forgotten that.
One does not mind,
Save when her shoes are thin,
And clouds behind.

What does it matter ? One
Forgets it : while
One keeps—her hair blown back,
Her eyes, her smile.

INNOCENCE

Now to praise Innocence,
That lonely flower,
That branch still out of reach,
That unspoilt hour,
That field, its weeds unsprung,
That day blue-skied,
That breeze blown fresh and cool,
That child clear-eyed.

Be wise and take a memory
Of scarcely heeded loveliness,
Glimpsed in a moment, suddenly,
Suddenly lost to sight.
Know it was lovely, and that he,
Who, in his eagerness,
Turns to make certain, turns to see
Can he repeat that swift delight,
Strives with the wind for mastery,
Loses it all or makes it less,
Finding perhaps not certainty,
Only distress.

Peasants my forebears were,
Say what you will ;
The peasant blood was there,
And lingers still.

The peasant's thrift and care,
His prudent toil,
His love of simple things,
And of the soil.

Their days were calmly spent,
Their nights were long ;
The joy they felt they'd hum
In some old song.

These are the men whose blood
Runs in my veins,
Well used to summer heat
And autumn rains.

Country physician, clerk,
Or clergyman,
It was the land they loved,
The land loved them.

Horses and dogs they held
As good as men,
Their pockets filled with crumbs
For some stray hen.

Books that were to their taste
They too would read ;
Speech was a luxury,
Silence a need.

And even I who seem
To break that line,
Have moments when I wish
A small field mine,

Will stop on sunny days
And pleasure feel
To see some fowl at work
On a dunghill.

Or in a doorway stand,
The dim cow-shed,
Pleasing me with its stalls
Where beasts are fed :

Watch them slow-munching now
Their share of hay,
Breathe the warm air they've breathed
Nor move away.

Can while a morning through
With this allure,
Or from a hill can watch
Them spread manure

Across a field from those
Small heaps near by,
Where the farm-cart had stopped
To let them lie.

These are the moments when
My heart makes free
To praise the very men
Who'd disown me,

To praise the very men
To whom a rhyme
That took a morning's work
Were waste of time.

THE BEQUEST

The gods who chose what each shall have
Before their birth, gave this to me,
That I should be a fool to wealth,
To beauty, and to constancy.

No money—no desire for it
(Some lovely face may make me long),
No fixed intent towards anything
More profitable than a song.

A poor bequest and they repent,
One gift deciding shall be mine :
That every woman, man, or child
I meet, is more to me than wine.

Let others cast a knife at fate,
Raging at what their fortune sends ;
I count them kind who chose my lot :
Made me a fool, but gave me friends.

STAR SPACES

The million stars that make the night
Are worlds in making, or else made :
This fable is not mine but those
Who better know how worlds are weighed.

A million stars, a thousand years
To reach the nearest, so they say,
That star's next comrade is to it
Five hundred thousand years away.

Come back to earth, forget these tales,
Give me three kisses, and then three :
Those lonely spaces have begot
A kindred loneliness in me.

THE TWO THINGS

Two things were born with me,
My heart to bother :
Wisdom was one of them,
Beauty the other.

It was not very long
Before I knew them ;
At first I loved, but then,
I learnt to rue them.

Wisdom laid hold of me,
Did me much kindness ;
Beauty was quick to give
Her lovely blindness.

Both were a joy to seek,
Both worth pursuing,
Both in a little time
Proved my undoing.

Wisdom, so sweet to-day,
Turned sad to-morrow ;
Beauty became an ache,
A smart, a sorrow.

One, pledging only truth,
Fled even from this ;
The other, promising all,
Broke every promise.

Who loves too zealously
Ends love with curses :
I never thought I'd live
To write such verses.

THE UNANSWERED RIDDLE

I've seen a child throw back his head
In joyous, half-astonished glee
At something suddenly made plain,
Some mystery.

I've seen him laugh, amazed to think
He had not thought of that before,
So simple was it in the end,
So true to law.

And I who ponder every day
A mystery more amazing still,
Hope always in the end to find
A principle ;

Some thread that runs through all the cloth,
Some truth that leaps to reconcile,
Some answer to unriddle all,
And make me smile.

Earth, this child,
Like a young tree,
Clean-limbed, very straight,
Deserves well of thee ;
See to it now that one
Joined perfectly,
So well begun, ends not
Ungracefully.

THE SINGERS

Sing, crickets, in the dusk,
About my caravan.
Sing loudly if you must,
Sweet, if you can.
Sing from that sandy soil
Where briers grow
To hide your little homes,
Not proud but low :
Sing where small roses wild,
Whose petals fall,
Rise sweetest in the dark
Not seen at all.
Sing for this summer's day,
Grown warm and long.
Sing for the very joy
There is in song.
Sing to the saffron sky
Streaked red, and soon,
When it has failed, sing on
To the pale moon.
Sing in that scented night
Invisibly,
And, as you always do,
Sing cheerfully.

A WOMAN

Spring was within the child's face, a cool freshness,
Afterwards summer, that most lovely thing ;
Autumn at last, mellow and very patient,
A lined beauty almost as beautiful as spring.

" Child, looking over the bog, what do you see, what
    have you seen all day ?
What dreams are given to you, here in this lonely, this
    lonely and lovely place ? "
" I see the brown, wet bog, and the misty hills, and the
    rain
Gathering on them to fall——" " And I—I see heaven
    within your face."

" No, stranger, not heaven. And you, where have you
    been who pass here,
Watching these ragged fields, these fields with the
    rock at war with the sod ? "
" I have been many places—bays, cities, and sun-
    scorched cliffs."
" You are a demi-god, stranger." " No, child, not a
    demi-god."

I know a girl who's like a flower,
So like that when I see her face,
I see one, all its unconcern,
And all its quiet, lovely grace.

She's shy, she's silent, she's apart,
She's grown to beauty as by stealth,
She's lightly swayed—a petal too
Has not her cheeks' more guarded wealth.

She's wistful, gentle, joyous, calm,
Her breath's a sigh she seems to take,
And in her eyes that mute appeal
That certain of her kindred make.

She'll lift her face to meet my own,
As flowers do in certain case,
And every time she does, I'll swear,
Another likeness I can trace

Of look, of poise, of turn of head,
Not far to seek, not hard to name
Between the two—but what's the use,
When every poet says the same?

IN EXILE

Who would have thought a little field,
   A patch of green where skies are wide,
The steep lane up a valley, and
   Smoke curling upwards from beside
Five lonely trees in that steep part,
Could stir such sadness in the heart?

Who would have thought a little field,
   A far-off road, a far-off lane,
A far-off cottage could in time
   Wake far-off thoughts with so much pain,
Wake far-off thoughts so hard to stem
A man might fear to think of them?

The bees are gone from the clover,
And the leaves are blown from the tree,
And I know a bird turns southward
In a brave certainty ;
And I know a bird will one day,
When the wind blows no less free,
Leaving the fields behind it,
Turn towards a vaster sea.

THE DUNGHILL

Against the shed's warm side the wood is piled,
Faggots heaped up in neat and even row ;
The sun pours down, the wall is pooled in sunlight,
Flies buzz, alight a moment, and then go.

Others upon the dunghill near by, hovering,
Hang poised in light, praising the warmer air ;
The whole heap comes to life, small gnats with gauze
    wings
Move on its surface quickly everywhere.

Around the heap hens scratch, two geese have mounted
Along the plank left for the barrow ; lo !
Full in the midst, content, they preen their feathers,
They bask, they close their eyes, they slumber now.

A cow stirs in its stall, a chain is rattled ;
One bird, deep-keeled, continues dosing ; one
Stretches its leg, stands up, then settles back on
This world newly awakened by the sun.

" Body, if worms permit of it,
Certainly into heaven you go,
Whiter than sheep's wool, if not quite
As white as snow.

" Warfare is ended, you have won,
Laurel and crown await you now.
Heaven is yours." " But Soul ? " " Alas !
Soul must remain below.

" Soul has betrayed the cause too oft,
Soul has looked backward every day,
Soul, while you held the narrow path,
Yearned for the broader way,

" Soul waging strife at midnight, soul
Wanton in lust and infamies,
Soul, that for each you miss, commits
Seven adulteries.

" Soul that cries grievance all the time,
Soul that asserts your virtue lie,
Soul that complains you murder joy,
Kindness, and innocency.

" Body, if worms permit of it,
Certainly into heaven you go,
Straightened this long time. Soul—alas !
Soul must remain below."

THE DISCOVERY

Adam, who thought himself immortal still,
Though cast from Eden, not knowing yet of death,
Nor guessing that what has beginning ends,
Nor that the life goes also with the breath,

Wandering in the empty fields one day,
Pushing the grass aside, finds Abel slain,
His arms thrown out, his head with briars twined,
And on the ground beside a dull red stain.

" Abel, it is not time for sleeping now ;
Have you forgot the curse upon us put ? "
So, standing by his side, he gazes down.
Thinking he jests, he stirs him with his foot.

Silence, no sound at all, a breathless calm ;
The warm day sighs ; its sighing does not last.
The grass-tops quiver slightly ; through the grass
A small field-mouse, disturbed, goes hurrying past.

Then, seized with sudden fear, he flings himself
Beside the corpse, cries, " For your mother's sake
Give me an answer. " Still no answer comes,
Only the cry, " Abel, awake, awake ! "

ANALOGY

So Hannah prayed unto the Lord,
Her lips a silent witnessing ;
But those around her never heard
Murmur, or stir, or whispering.

They only saw her lips that moved,
They saw her eyes that gave no sign,
They saw a look of blank despair ;
And thought it was the work of wine.

None of them knew what anguish stirred
Within that eager, pleading brain ;
None of them knew what bitterness
Gave to her heart its duller pain.

But I can guess it ; I can tell ;
I know that emptiest of ways ;
I know that void—so poets feel
To whom no poem comes for days.

SEVEN EPIGRAMS

Too many now lament the times grown evil,
See only clouds across the pallid moon,
For all these night-owls hooting fear so often
Give me one cockerel greeting dawn too soon.

To Socrates returned, one stopped, made answer,
" Look in the air, and see there highways strange ;
Look in the earth, and see how deep men burrow."
" And the soul ? "—" Socrates, souls do not change."

Since all can travel, each returns to show
His boots from Burmah, hat from Tennessee,
His necktie purchased in the booths at Delhi,
And his religion patch-work from all three.

Of nine men met, eight tell me, when I meet them,
War is the one thing they will never swallow.
The fence seems sure, but do not worry, Cæsar,
Once the first sheep has jumped the rest will follow.

Struck with soul-sickness, Modernus has hastened
To Nux, the mind physician, to be whole.
One devil cast, seven entered—he's instructed
That he was wrong and that he has no soul.

Pity that author who in ten years time
Attempts to win his book a modest sale ;
Incest, adultery so well exploited,
There's nothing left to make a brave, proud tale.

While Dives, full of meats and doubting, ponders,
" Have I, or have I not, indeed, a soul ? "
Lazarus, well aware at least of one thing,
Wonders how body best may be kept whole.

THE BALANCE

In the night when men can see
More than the day reveals to eye,
I saw an angel weighing earth's
Many-toned and varied cry.

In one scale the fears, the dread,
The blood-wrung sobs that rise with pain ;
In the other hope and joy
And courage come to life again.

" Cast in the bliss that children feel,
Cast in their laughter now," I cried ;
" Terror and blows and helplessness
Cast in," a voice replied.

" Cast in the thoughts that come with spring,
The summer's long, late-houred calm " ;
" Cast winter in, the cold that nips,
The hungry stomach's icy balm."

" All gentle and all kindly thoughts,
All comforts shared, all pity shed."
" Those jagged strips of steel that tear
Another's flesh, cast in," they said.

So did the scales tip up and down,
First one, then other was before.
" Which wins ? " I called, and suddenly—
Dawn, and I saw no more.

CHARLES CHAPLIN IN
"THE GOLD RUSH"

I have made more men laugh than Rabelais ;
For one that in the theatre at Athens
Saw Socrates in mid-air in his basket
Nine hundred saw and laughed at me to-day.

Only the lean Spaniard, long in prison,
Brought joy and sorrow to be so close neighbours,
Made the absurd seem sad, the sad seem foolish—
But he used two, I have used only one.

FRENCH PEASANTS

These going home at dusk
Along the lane,
After the day's warm work,
Do not complain.

Were you to say to them,
" What does it mean ?
What is it all about,
This troubled dream ? "

They would not understand,
They'd go their way,
Or, if they spoke at all,
They'd surely say,

" Dawn is the time to rise,
Days are to earn
Bread and the mid-day rest,
Dusk to return ;

" To be content, to pray.
To hear songs sung,
Or to make wayside love,
If one is young.

" All from the good God comes,
All then is good ;
Sorrow is known to Him,
And understood."

One who had questioned all,
And was not wise,
Might be ashamed to meet
Their quiet eyes.

All is so clear to them,
All is so plain,
These who go home at dusk,
Along the lane.

THE CHERRY TREES

Trees in the snow,
Who would know
Your branches bare
Will one day grow
Green buds again,
Lovely with rain
Where now a ridge
Of snow has lain?
Who would surmise
What beauty lies
Hidden in you,
Till winter dies?
All now is dead,
Your grace is fled
Save when the moon
Shines overhead.
Boughs stript and bare
Lift to the air
Their twisted arms
As though in prayer.
A cloak of white
Hides out of sight
Grass where will fall
Petals most light.
Nothing to show,
No one to know
Your miracle,
Trees in the snow.

ON A HILL

In the dark one night
I stopped to hear
Some quiet beast that grazed
In a field near.

It made a stealthy sound
In that still gloom,
At first I heard it, then
I saw it loom

Up in a corner where
It softly fed ;
It moved along the hedge
Nor raised its head.

It never raised its head,
It breathed the dew ;
The stars were out that night,
A low mist too.

Along the hedge it came.
I stood like stone.
I thought of all those hours
It passed alone,

ON A HILL

Up in that fragrant dark
From dusk till when
The fainter streaks of dawn
Showed forth again.

No sound came to that place,
No step would pass ;
The vaulted sky was clear
And cool the grass.

I thought, though fools despise
This foolish beast,
A man might envy it
The night at least.

The sea cries to the land, " You have taken from me
The one garland I had, to spread on your fields ;
Nothing to you that it dries and shrinks in the sun
So long as your crop another measure yields."

And the land replies, " Miser, you grudge me this ?
This one beggarly gift from your grasp that slips ?
How much have you taken from me, who talk now of
    theft ?
Lovers, and little children, and strong men, and
    ships."

THE ELYSIAN FIELDS

O lovely fields, though none now sing you,
I sing you now in this late time,
Suddenly, as a man remembering
Out of its season and its clime
A copse whose leaves are green and do not fall,
Some sunlit country pleasant to recall.

Let all go past, it does not touch me,
I linger still, fixed to the ground,
Turned back to a forgotten hillside,
Brooding on it like one spell-bound,
Whose friends go on, who still remains behind,
And means to turn, and turns indeed in mind.

So have I turned, O lovely meadows,
So have I felt your call again,
So have I stood and brooded on you,
So have I known a joy half pain,
An exile joy a man might almost fear,
An exile joy that brings the far-off near.

Beauty like yours is not discarded,
Though all forget you, one recalls,
Though all deny you, I affirm you,
Though all ignore you, one extols
Pastures where head may lie and heart can rest,
Grass very cool and long and quite unprest.

I shall come yet, at dusk it may be,
Up some long creek to some calm pool,
And see those slopes still warm with sunlight
And feel that breeze blown freshly cool,
From hedges that do not depend on spring,
Orchards in which a bird may always sing.

ANOTHER FIELD

Within the mind's fair field this morn I saw
Flocks of small birds, that, like a shower of rain,
Fell to the earth, and chattered gaily there,
While some into the sky arose again.

Till noon, and then a crowd of sooty daws,
Black as hell's mouth must be, espied the mound,
Settled upon it and within a trice
Not one of those dawn greeters could be found.

Black deed, black throng. Would that a Voice might
    come
And scatter such drab bastards to the wind.
Come, little singers, cleave the sky once more,
Cover the grass, search through its blades, and find.

A NORTHERN TOWN

I can remember in a town
I lived in once, I shall not say
How long, for I'd forget it now—
Its streets of grey

Hard to the foot, its dust, its noise,
Its tired people when night falls,
Their very laughter shrill and hard,
Its music-halls ;

Its churches shaken by the street,
Its parks, its posters, and its signs,
Its shops where dirty cards were sold,
Its tramway lines,

All of it ugly, until spring,
Coming one day when I was there,
The trees along more quiet streets
Felt the mild air,

Broke into leaf, and chestnuts tall,
Until that moment scarcely seen,
Spilt on the pavement shade from leaves
Marvellously green.

And children on their way from school,
Dull and sedately clothed before,
Scenting the spring as had the trees,
Suddenly wore

Blue linen dresses—oh, so blue,
Bluer than any summer sky,
And white straw hats with crimson bands,
That caught the eye.

I tell you that whole town was changed
For one at least on that same day,
Losing its ugliness, become
No longer grey,

But splashed with colour as one went,
Patches of green, a glint of blue
Against the street and instantly
The street was new.

Never were children more delight
Than in the mornings these to me,
Hurrying past, their satchels swung
Against their knee.

Or, if at evening one walked home,
Some suburb road, when rain had been
To cool the pavement, never trees
Seemed half so clean,

Or half so fresh, or half so cool,
Or thickly spread, as those that grew
Along the curb, with tender leaves
The light showed through.

Beauty, that will not be denied,
If I have doubted anything,
Call to my mind a certain town,
A certain spring.

OUTSKIRTS OF PARIS

In the train
I once saw
A woman singing
To her lover.

Bareheaded,
Her black hair
Held from her forehead
With a comb.

Young, eager,
Her very smile
Held more
Than another's laughter.

It is Sunday,
They go to the country ;
In some green place
They will rest a while.

As she sings
I am made lonely ;
She rests her hand
Against his knee,

And they sing together
Some sweet song
Known only
To their own people.

I have read many books ;
Not one of them
Gave me the joy
This woman gave me.

GIRL WITH WASHING-BASKET

Your eyes most grave and brown,
Your far-off gaze,
Not of the town indeed
In these strange days.

They look beyond the throng,
Their thoughts are slow ;
What place they see, what dreams
I do not know.

What hopes they have, what joy,
What sorrow too :
All this, if it is known,
Is known to few.

But I who see you now,
Bareheaded, see
That by that fact you come
From the country.

Some farm, some distant spot,
Some lonely place ;
I wish that village well
For your calm face.

I wish that village well,
Whose cloudless skies,
Whose quiet fields at dusk
Made your mild eyes.

Your thoughts, your hidden hopes,
I cannot tell,
But, if one thinks of you—
I wish him well.

CONTRAST

Once in a city I have heard
The noise continue close on dawn,
Until that time when birds begin
Singing to greet the coming morn.

Then for a moment all was still,
The traffic ceased, the roar died down,
Five minutes passed, and not a wheel
Troubled the pavement of that town.

Five minutes passed, while every place
Where men had slept the whole night long
In leafy stillness, cool with dew,
Woke with a sudden burst of song.

THE BETRAYAL

I am betrayed by love, who promised me
Many sweet songs, if I would leave her side,
But for one day, and underneath that tree,
Where the shades deepest and most cool abide,
For a few hours with my pen—Good God,
My pen writes swifter than I can, and all
It writes are rhymes and little roundelays,
Fit to make kites for children in the spring,
Songs stolen from the poets I recall,
But not one poem for the child I sing.

REMINISCENCE

If I should speak to you of one
I knew indeed five years ago,
And of the sweet look in her face,
And of her calm and lovely brow,
Her smile that was a child's smile too,
Her youth which made her grave or gay,
Her sudden mirth, her seriousness,
Her open gaze from eyes most grey
Looking beyond the thing ; her poise,
The turn of head, her laughter shy,
And that grave earnestness which gave
All that she did serenity ;
If I should praise, as praise I should,
I think that you who never saw
Even the street in which she lived,
The chestnut tree, the path, the door,
The narrow window-box above
The dusty road, its noise still clear,
That roof which sheltered all I loved,
And those five steps which brought her near,
If I could praise, I think that you,
Knowing not her, nor I who rhyme,
Struck by the wonder of my words,
Would read them through a second time.

I tell her she is lovely, and she laughs,
Shy laughter altogether lovely too,
Knowing, perhaps, that it was true before,
And, when she laughs, that it is still more true.

SONG

Singer within the little streets,
Sing her a song about a fool who came,
Looked in her eyes, and in that moment knew
Nothing would be the same

Ever again, a fool who hardly knew
When the stars shone, or when the slanting rain,
Beat on his face, or anything at all,
Or any pain

Save the one pain—to-morrow might not come,
Or any fear—save that he should be blind,
Or any thought—save that her words were sweet,
Her eyes were kind.

I said I will not turn aside
Though beauty pass me in my stride ;
Though beauty pass me in the way
I will not heed her once to-day ;
That sudden joy, that swifter pain,
That stab within the heart again ;
That leaping-up, that quickening fire,
That almost-anguish, that desire ;
That unattainable, that snare,
That all that beauty is, despair ;
That nothingness, that fantasy,
That broken promise—meant to be ;
That breeze blown nowhere, that sweet stir,
That scorn of the philosopher,
I will not heed, I will not see,
I will not pause amazedly ;
I will not stop, swing round, delay ;
Though beauty pass one yard away,
I will not even turn my head,
Though beauty brush my sleeve, I said :
All this I said, and more I'd learned,
And beauty passed me—and I turned !

She who was always laughing
Is silent now,
Fearing to meet my eyes,
Lest they should show
Something not there before,
And all I know
Is that what's lost was lovely,
Is that I grow
To say, give back her laughter,
And let love go.

REMORSE

I might have been a poet still,
I might be singing carelessly,
Had someone not come up one day
And sown philosophy

Within my heart—a little seed,
Too small you'd think to do much wrong,
And yet it grew till presently
It came to stifle song ;

Casting so long a shadow on
The grass, where poets like to sing,
That even love, that seemed so sweet,
Became a foolish thing.

And all those happy, empty thoughts
That leap to life when one is young,
Were turned to folly on my lips,
Before they could be sung.

And, though a tune's of little count,
And knowledge more than all to me,
Who knows what music may have died
When that small seed fell silently ?

FROM DISCIPLE TO MASTER

My life is like a dream :
I do not know
How it began, nor yet
How it will go.

Out of the night a bird
Has quickly flown
Across the lighted room,
And now is gone

Into the dark again
From whence it came,
So the old Druids said,
And I, the same.

But we are not content,
I, like them too,
Questioning all I meet,
Seek something new.

Saying to each who comes,
" So much is clear,
But if you know of more,
I wait to hear.

" The dark, the lighted room,
The bird which flies
Are not enough for man
Who one day dies.

Are not enough for man
That bird which came
Out of the dark and must
Return again.

" If you know more besides,
Tell what you know,
O wise and travelled souls,
Before I go."

A MOTHER

Unto the world
This woman gives
That which alone
Unending lives.

Nothing is here
But has its springs
Set in the first
And source of things.

Nothing is here
That may not go
Further than man
Or stars can know.

Her hour come,
She forged in pain
Part of a yet
Unbroken chain.

This is the past
Reborn once more,
This is the future
Held in store.

Now in her arms
She holds indeed
Sowing and harvest,
Fruit and seed.

So I, whose words
Must fail with time,
Praise her within
A barren rhyme.

THE HOUSE

Presently, when the stir
Dies in the little street,
When I no longer heed
Chatter, or passing feet ;

When I have learnt to use
Window, and door, and bolt,
How to outwit the knave,
How to expel the dolt ;

No longer mocked by lies,
No longer prey to fool,
No longer tyrannised,
I shall begin to rule.

Too much confusion now,
Too wild a discontent,
Too many voices heard,
Servants grown insolent ;

Time to assert the will,
Time to make clear my choice,
Time to begin to speak
With a more certain voice.

Ordered at last throughout,
Ridden of bat and mouse,
Presently, I shall be
Master in my own house.

THE BEES

Then to the bees one said,
" Knowledge from us is fled ;
The stream is grown impure,
Nought that we say is sure ;
The cloud of doubt clouds all,
Rain has begun to fall.

Come you, unto our aid,
Come, sages, honey-fed ;
You who roam far and wide,
Many-winged, many-eyed.
Who, out of all your sort,
Show the most anxious thought,
Building the sixfold cell
Wondrously, very well ;
You, who in honeyed dark
Brood on the mystery stark
Of birth and death and pain
And of re-birth again,
See summer follow spring
And autumn winter bring,
For whom were these things done ?
For whom still shines the sun ?
For whom does dew descend ?
For whom the winter end ?
Is it not all for men ?
Make our minds proud again.

Are we not last of things?
Have we not also wings,
And do we not one day
Spread them and pass away?"

His little friends replied,
"Wisdom with you has died.
Only the bees have souls.
Even in trees and holes
Of wood the wild bees know
More than your words now show.
Is not the world a field
Spread in the sun to yield
Honey and scent and dew,
Its share of labour too?
Is not night sent to cool
The too-warm liquid pool
Of golden sweetness, day
Only to show the way
To lonely flowers which
Hide in a far-off ditch?

"And is not heaven indeed
Rather another mead,
Untouched by time, unseen,
A hedge for ever green,
Seasonless, always spring
And early summer, a thing

71

Hid in the future, yet
Surer than autumns wet?
This is our hope, and we
Hold it in certainty
Though the hive leak and though
Winter and rain and snow
Break through the vaulting high
And send us out to die
Wingless upon the hill,
That field awaits us still,
And from the yellow sod
The bees return to God."

HUMILITY FOR POETS

Of all the cocks that greeted dawn to-day
How many will be heard a year from now?
How many preen their feathers on the heap,
How many strut the yard, how many crow?

So when I see the thousand voices raised
To catch their audience by the printed line,
Is it not folly to believe that one,
Sounding a twelve-month hence, may yet be mine?

No woman now
Can make me turn,
Make temple throb,
Or heart to burn.
Though she have grace,
Though she have charm,
Though she have beauty,
It's no harm.
I'll wish her joy
And go my way,
Neither regret
Nor yet delay.
Her lips are not
For mine I know :
Once I'd have wondered,
Now I go.
I take my road
Without vain sighs,
Kept by the thought
Of other eyes,
Kinder than any,
Clear and cool,
Steadfast as star
And calm as pool :
Kept by the thought
Of all that's shown
Hidden in them
To meet my own.

So might a man,
Who walks at night,
Pass without heeding
Each stray light,
Hold on his course,
Though far he roam,
Scornful of inns,
At thought of home.

CHILDREN

These wayfarers
From another country,
These wanderers
Knowing not all.

What shall we say to them,
Who have brought with them
So much wonder
In their eyes?

Say nothing,
Nothing we can say
Can add to what
They have already.

They have joy,
They have the morning,
And they have wonder
In their eyes.

These wayfarers
From another country,
These wanderers
Knowing not all.

GODS

The gods are dead they tell us now,
None walk the earth as they once did.
Yet each may be a god who wills,
And none prevent him, none forbid.

A penny given to a child
Can turn a sky of grey to gold,
Two pennies given make his heart
Leap with the joy of wealth untold.

Now am I Mercury if I wish,
Now am I Zeus if I so chose,
Now can I bring Olympus down
To this next mortal lacking shoes.

He passes me, the chance is gone,
The god's wing'd feet o'erlook his need,
Olympus clouds again with mist :
What men proclaim is true indeed.

Kneel, little child, to God
And thank Him for the trees,
That are a home to birds,
That are an inn to bees ;
That are a joy to all
When on the ground they shed
Patches of cool, dark shade
Under a tired head ;
That are a friend to you,
When in a field you lie,
Face downwards to the earth,
Face upwards to the sky.
Lie there and thank Him, and,
If dusty feet should pass,
Kneel, little child, to God
And thank Him for the grass.

THE THOUGHT

When I was still a boy, no more,
They stole my youth, that is to say,
I got, what other men must wait,
Knowledge and sorrow in a day.

How came it does not matter here,
Some quarrel between moneyed men,
And I was luckier than most,
Though what I gained was bitter then.

But now it pleases me to think
That, though it's lost, the debt is due,
And I can give, what still is mine,
Of lovely hope and ardour too.

So that I never see a child
Go past me with a joy that cures
All bitter feeling, but I think,
" Ah, little one, my youth is yours ! "

Now at this season, Love, who's wise,
Knowing his time must surely come,
Sets in her face a signal sweet,
Denied to some.

If she was fair before, she'll now
Suddenly into beauty spring,
If she was young, he'll add to that
Another thing.

All her shy grace will seem to come
Out of an eagerness within,
And in her face the colour mount
To warm her skin.

Never before or after quite
Will she be as she is to-day ;
Love, who is wise, has seen to that,
To have his way.

THE GARDEN

Then in the night when men
Remember former pain,
Remember the past years
And their lost hopes and fears,
The wounds from which they've bled,
Their tears shed and unshed,
And folly too, while some
Dread more the years to come,—
Suddenly, without cause,
Those thoughts were given pause,
And, like a lovely face,
I thought of you, green place !
I thought of that steep lane,
Narrow, and wet from rain,
Its great stone flags, its two
Walls screening out from view
What lies behind the straight
Iron and ivied gate.
O garden after rain,
I saw your paths again.
I saw the fresh brown earth
Bringing small plants to birth ;
Lettuces young and clean,
Neat rows of tender green.
I saw the things that bring
Tokens indeed of spring,
Shoots that would soon unfold
Others their secret told,
Rich leafage newly grown,
Walls wherein seeds were sown,

Borders with dark tiles set,
And a stray violet,
Patches of clover and
Those flowers unhelp'd by hand,
Weeds far too beautiful
For one to stoop and pull.
O garden after rain,
I saw your paths again.
Immediately such calm
Fell on my soul like balm,
It was as if I stood
In that fresh, shady rood ;
So that I wondered how
A place could move me now,
Stronger in memory
Than if it met the eye.
And as I lay and let
Memory draw its net
About that sheltered spot,
Lovely, expected not,
Peace from its well-filled store
Stole on me more and more,
My darker thoughts were dead,
Doubt and despair had fled,
And in their place I knew
Patience and hope anew.

OF ONE WHO HAS BEAUTY

She who has one thing only,
And that one thing so well,
That, when they see her passing,
All hearts must tell,
All hearts must pay her tribute ;
One heart may sometimes bring
Regret, that they who gave it,
Gave but one thing.

THE DENIAL

I have denied my love ;
I said to her,
" Three days now and I bring
My best song to you,
As yet unwritten."

Five days now I have waited,
And all my words
Are words of fools and rhymers ;
Love, if I do return,
It will be empty-handed.

SOME LINES ON AN OLD SUBJECT

She gave her mouth, as fresh as dawn,
As sweet as spring, as cool as dew,
To meet my own, and when they met,
It seemed my own was new.

It seemed my own was new to feel
Some little breeze blown straight from June,
A moment's warmth, or that it touched
A flower closed too soon.

If I have kissed before to-day,
Those kisses are forgotten now,
And if I kiss like this again,
Only her lips will know.

FRATRICIDE

Lust has slain his brother Love,
He whose feet were meant to run
Lightly on the mountain tops
And greet the rising of the sun.

Now Love is dead and heavy Lust
Broods in the valley far below,
Sullen to think of those high peaks
Where he himself can never go.

O hapless Love, unhappy Lust :
Mourn both for slayer and for slain,
For he who kills that light-foot youth
Brings him not back to life again.

THE LITTLE FIELD

Within a little field
A man may find
A pleasant place to lie
And rest his mind ;
A sheltered, sloping bank,
Grass cool and long ;
So beauty may be hedged
In a small song.

We have hardened our hearts within us, our hearts
    are grown very hard ;
Hard words in our mouths are spoken, hard are the
    roads we tread ;
We have forgotten softness ; we have put by those
    things ;
Hard days, hard nights before us—and a hard bed.

The five steps up to a doorway, a path through the
    fields at dusk,
Hard thoughts have taken their places, hard are the
    jests we make ;
All that might bring remembrance, all that might wake
    regret,
Our hearts are hardened against them—lest they
    should break.

PROSE POEMS

YOUTH

Go not out of that meadow for a little time, for there are many flowers to be gathered in it that you will not find elsewhere, and the stream, made drowsy by the pleasant day, flows smoothly through it, and along the hedges there is sweet shade and the cool grass. And, though the road over the hill shines bravely in the distance, be sure that there is much dust upon it and feet grow tired soon, and, further, once one has taken it, there is no returning here.

Take my songs. Take my songs, for there are only a few words to them, and words are soon read and in a little time forgotten. If I had been busy in the market-place, or if I had spent my days in bending others to my will ; or if I had even been content to make a living out of hearsay wisdom, giving again what was given to me, and repeating again what had come to me on other lips, you would have understood. But I have done none of these things. I have wasted my days.

What one gave to the market-place, or what another gave to the government of the people, I have given to a few words. Others went up and took the citadel by force. I was not there. Others waited for the falling tide, and sailed their ships upon it. I watched them go. Others flung roses in hill-side gardens, and laughed, and found an answering laughter to their own. I remained silent.

All have gone past me in the street, and I have turned aside into a narrow lane, where there is no noise, and where all day long the sun casts lazy shadows on the quiet stones ; where the air is still, and where no sound comes, and where the drowsy pigeons make no disturbance along the top of the grass-tufted wall.

Take my songs, for there are only a few words to them, and words are soon read, and in a little time forgotten.

TIME OF HAWTHORN

Girl with the shining eyes, what do you know of love ?

It is as though you had stopt, head bent, lips parted, and were listening for something. That little wind blown about the hawthorn trees is not enough to hold you. Why, then, do you stop, why do you wait, shyly eager one moment, half afraid the next, as though to catch the sound of some word not yet spoken ? Why do you turn your head ?

I know your secret. It is not the warm morning, nor the sun that is shining in your hair, nor those white clouds drifting across a blue sky, nor is it the sweet freshness in the air, nor the scent of the blossom, nor the songs along the hedges, that have given your cheeks their delicately-shaded loveliness, or made your face eager, or your hands restless ; but it is some wildness stirring in your own heart, that you have hidden from the world, some foolishness that has strayed into your thoughts and that is holding them at all times and in all places.

For what do you wait ? What are you listening for ? Is it love ? What is it that has made your days like a dream, and your nights like a soft whisper under the quiet stars ? Is it love ?
Is it love ?

Girl with the shining eyes, it is because you know nothing of love, that your eyes are shining.

SAD SONGS

I could have written you many sad songs if you had asked me at one time, for there was a time when sorrow passed nearer to me than you think, and when my mind was for ever wandering in unhappy places. But those things are better not spoken of, and those songs are as well left unsung : and, though it might even have been given them to draw tears from many eyes, there need be no regret : there is enough sorrow for all of us without writing of it, and it is better in the end that it should be forgotten.

OF CERTAIN VERSES

Old verses I have no pleasure in you ;
All that you say is finished with long ago ;
Leaves damped with the many rains of autumn
Are like the moods we no longer know :
Henceforth my verses are to be different,
Sprung from the soil, but impatiently,
Clean, straight, fresh, and like arrows pointed—
Green blades under an April sky.

CERTAIN OF THE POEMS IN THIS BOOK
HAVE APPEARED IN *The Branch of
Hawthorn Tree* IN A LIMITED EDITION
ISSUED BY THE GRAYHOUND PRESS, WITH
ILLUSTRATIONS BY THE FRENCH ARTIST,
PICART LE DOUX